Greenville Collins & Clifton

Secrets of the trade

For watchmakers and jewelers

Greenville Collins & Clifton

Secrets of the trade
For watchmakers and jewelers

ISBN/EAN: 9783337135393

Printed in Europe, USA, Canada, Australia, Japan

Cover: Foto ©Lupo / pixelio.de

More available books at **www.hansebooks.com**

SECRETS OF THE TRADE.

FOR

WATCHMAKERS AND JEWELERS.

*These formulæ and recipes have been gathered
from the most reliable sources, and can be
thoroughly recommended by the authors.*

COLLINS & CLIFTON,

MANUFACTURING JEWELERS AND WATCHMAKERS.

GREENVILLE, S. C.

"Southern School for Watchmakers and Jewelers."

JUNE, 1892.

1892:
SHANNON & Co., Printers and binders,
Greenville, S. C.

PREFACE.

The object of writing this text book is to place before the Jobbers, Watchmakers, Jewelers and Horological Schools a treatise that can be of some use and thoroughly relied upon by all the branches of the trade. Having spent considerable time over this work we hope and trust that it will meet with all the requirements it is purposed to. Trusting that our endeavors have not been lost on the immense area of the United States, and, on the other hand, that they will be appreciated, we remain yours respectfully,

COLLINS & CLIFTON,

"Southern School for Watchmakers and Jewelers."

INTRODUCTION.

We wish to state to our readers that, in all the following recipes, it is absolutely necessary to employ the use of pure chemicals, unless otherwise stated, and that, should any of our recipes *not* be fully understood, we would be most pleased to make them so on receipt of a self-addressed envelope; and further, that the weights and measures are perfectly exact. Care must be exercised in compounding and mixing solutions, powders, etc., being careful to keep from inhaling the fumes and vapors given forth by the chemical action of any of the substances which may be used or operated upon. In filtering solutions, etc., a common glass funnel with a little fine cotton pressed into the neck may be used to advantage, being the most economical filter that we know of.

SECRETS OF THE TRADE.

CHAPTER I.

ALLOYS.

Gold alloys for enamelling or lapping :

Gold	1 oz.	
Silver	9 dwts.	
Copper	2 "	

Gold . .	1 oz.	
Silver . .	9 dwts.	
Copper . .	3 "	12 grs.

Gold	1 oz.	
Silver	10 dwts.	
Copper	3 "	12 grs.

Gold	1 oz.	
Silver	1 dwt.	12 gr.
Copper	2 "	12 "

Gold	1 oz.	
Silver	9 dwt.	12 gr.
Copper	7 "	12 "

Gold	1 oz.	
Silver	14 dwts.	
Copper	8 "	

Gold	2 ozs.	5 dwts.
Silver	1 oz.	6 "
Copper		5 "
Pin Brass		5 "

Gold	1 oz.	
Silver	12 dwts.	
Copper	6 "	

Enamelling gold for transparent enamelling :

Gold . . . . 1 oz.
Silver . . . . 14 dwts.
Copper . . . . 6 "

Gold . . . . 1 oz.
Silver . . . . 1 dwt. 20 grs.
Copper . . . . 1 "   4 "

18k Pale Gold . . . . 1 oz.
Silver . . . . 4 dwts.
Copper . . . . 2 "   15 grs.

18k Gold . . . . 1 oz. 12 grs.
Silver . . . . 3 dwts. 8 grs.
Copper . . . . 3 "   8 "

Alloys for best gold pens :

Gold . . . . 1 oz.
Silver . . . . 5 dwts.
Copper . . . . 7 "   18 grs.
Spelter . . . . 1 "   6 "

Gold . . . . 1 oz.
Composition . . . . 1 "   13 dwts.

Composition for the above :

Silver . . . . 1 oz. 17 dwts.
Copper . . . . • . . . . 5 "   15 "
Spelter . . . . 18 dwts. 20 grs.

Gold . . . . 1 oz.
Silver . . . . 2 "
Copper . . . . 1 "

Yellow gold :

Gold . . . . 1 oz.
Silver . . . . 5 dwts. 6 grs.
Copper . . . . 3 "   12 "
Pin Brass . . . . 18 "

Gold . . . . 1 oz.
Silver . . . . 4 dwts.
Copper . . . . 4 "
Pin Brass . . . . 16 "

Gold . . . . 1 oz.
Silver . . . . 5 dwts. 12 grs.
Copper . . . . 3 "   12 "
Pin Brass . . . . 19 "   6 "

Gold . . . . 1 oz.
Silver . . . . 3 dwts. 21 grs.
Copper . . . . 9 "   3 "
Composition . . . . 5 "   6 "

Gold . . . . 15 dwts. 9 grs.
Silver . . . . 5 "   19 "
Copper . . . . 3 "   21 "
Composition . . . . 15 "

Composition for the above :
  Copper . . . . 1 oz.
  Spelter . . . . 5 dwts.

In making solder for the foregoing, always take of the alloyed gold you are using, 1 dwt., silver 12 grs.

Handy Table of Alloys—Different Qualities of Gold.

QUALITY.	FINE GOLD.			COMPOSITION.			TOTAL.		
	Oz.	Dwts.	Grs.	Oz.	Dwts.	Grs.	Oz.	Dwt.	Gr.
9 karat	0	7	12	0	12	12	1	0	0
12 "	0	10	0	0	10	0	1	0	0
15 "	0	12	12	0	7	12	1	0	0
18 "	0	15	0	0	5	0	1	0	0
22 "	0	18	18	0	1	6	1	0	0

Composition for the above :

Silver	3 ozs.	5 dwts.	12 grs.
Copper	8 "	12 "	12 "
Spelter	1 "	18 "	6 "

Bright gold, 9k :

Gold . . . . 1 oz.
Silver . . . . 7 dwts.
Composition . . . . 1 oz. 6 dwts.

Gold, 8k :

Gold . . . . 1 oz.
Silver . . . . 8 dwts.
Composition . . . . 1 oz. 12 dwts.

Composition for making 9k gold for above :

Copper . . . . 44 ozs.
Spelter . . . . 8 "

Gold, 8k :

Gold . . . . 5 dwts.
Silver . . . . 3 " 6 grs.
Copper . . . . 6 " 12 "

California :

Gold . . . . 11 ozs.
Composition . . . . 15 " 10 dwts.

Composition for California :

Silver . . . . 15 ozs. 12 dwts.
Copper . . . . 67 "
Spelter . . . . 11 "

Spelter alloy :

8k gold . . . . 1 oz. 13 dwts. 6 grs.
Silver . . . . 1 " 12 " 12 "
Copper . . . . 1 " 12 " 6 "
Spelter . . . . 4 "

How to make any karat gold from fine 24k gold:

EXAMPLE.—Suppose you have 70 dwts. of fine gold and desire to make 14k. You should proceed as follows:

70 dwts. the weight,
24k the quality.

1680 number of dwts. of 1k.

14)1680(120 number of dwts. of 24k.
    70   "   "   "   "   "

50 alloy to be added.

If you wish to use American gold, multiply the weight by 21 3-5k, or if you use sovereigns, multiply the weight by 22k.
You can make these alloys in ozs., dwts. or grs.

18k French alloy :
Gold . . . . 150 parts.
Silver . . . . 23 "
Copper . . . . 27 "

18k Red :
Gold . . . . 90 parts.
Silver . . . . 5 "
Copper . . . . 25 "

16k gold :
Gold . . . . 64 parts
Silver . . . . 15 "
Copper . . . . 17 "

16k red gold :
Gold . . . . 64 parts.
Silver . . . . 7 "
Copper . . . . 25 "

14k gold :
Gold . . . . 140 parts.
Silver . . . . 40 "
Copper . . . . 60 "

14k red:

Gold	70 parts.
Silver	10 "
Copper	40 "

12k gold:

Gold	120 parts.
Silver	50 "
Copper	70 "

12k red gold:

Gold	120 parts.
Silver	30 "
Copper	90 "

10k gold:

Gold	100 parts.
Silver	60 "
Copper	80 "

12k red gold:

Fine gold	12 dwts.
Copper	12 "

White gold:

Gold	12 dwts.
Silver	12 "

Green gold:

Gold	19 parts.
Silver	5 "

18k green gold:

Gold	1 oz.
Silver	6 dwts. 6 grs.

19k green gold:

Gold	5 dwts.
Silver	1 " 12 grs.

16k red gold :
Gold . . . . 5 dwts.
Copper . . . . 2 " 12 grs.

20k red gold :
Gold . . . . 5 dwts.
Copper . . . . 1 " 6 grs.

17k gold :
Gold . . . . 15 dwts.
Silver . . . . 1 " 10 grs.
Copper . . . . 4 " 17 "

18k gold :
Gold . . . . 1 oz.
Silver . . . . 4 dwts. 10 grs.
Copper . . . . 2 " 5 "

18k gold :
Gold . . . . 15 dwts.
Silver . . . . 2 " 4 grs.
Copper . . . . 2 " 19 "

18k gold :
Gold . . . . 18 dwts,
Silver . . . . 2 " 18 grs.
Copper . . . . 3 " 18 "

18k gold :
Gold . . . . 1 oz. 1 dwt. 6 grs.
Silver . . . . 3 dwts. 10 grs.
Copper . . . . 4 " 12 "

19k gold :
Gold . . . . 1 oz.
Silver . . . . 2 dwts. 6 grs.
Copper . . . . 3 " 12 "'

20k gold :
        Gold . . . . 1 oz.
        Silver . . . . 2 dwts.
        Copper . . . . 2 "   4 grs.

12k gold :
        Gold . . . . 18 dwts.
        Silver . . . . 12 "
        Copper . . . . 1 "   3 grs.

17k gold :
        Gold . . . . 1 dwt.
        Silver . . . . 6 grs.

15k gold :
        Gold · · . . . . · · . 1 oz.
        Silver . . . . 3 dwts. 12 grs.
        Copper . . . . 9 "

14k gold :
        Gold . . . . 1 oz.
        Silver . . . . 4 dwts.
        Copper . . . . 9 "   12 grs.

14k gold :
        Gold . . . . 1 oz.
        Silver . . . . 4 dwts. 12 grs.
        Copper . . . . 10 "

13k gold :
        Gold . . . . 1 oz.
        Silver . . . . 4 dwts. 12 grs.
        Copper . . . . 10 "   12 "

13k gold :
        Gold . . . . 1 oz.
        Silver . . . . 6 dwts.
        Copper . . . . 8 "

13k gold :
    Gold . . . . 1 oz.
    Silver . . . . 4 dwts. 12 grs.
    Copper . . . . 10 "   12 "

14k gold :
    Gold . . . . 1 oz.
    Silver . . . . 8 dwts.
    Copper . . . . 4 "

15k gold :
    Gold . . . . 1 oz. 18 dwts.
    Silver . . . . 12 dwts. 12 grs.
    Copper . . . . 10 "

Extra color—16k gold :
    Gold . . . . 1 oz.
    Silver . . . . 6 dwts.
    Copper . . . . 4 "

Blue gold :
    Fine gold . . . . 18 dwts.
    Iron . . . . 6 "

7k gold :
    Copper . . . . 9 ozs.
    Silver . . . . 8 "
    Gold . . . . 7 "

Gray gold :
    Fine gold . . . . 16 dwts. 16 grs.
    Iron charcoal . . . . 3 "   8 "

Melting Points of Gold, Etc.

    23k will melt at . . . . 2 012° Fahr.
    22k "   " " . . . . 2 009° "
    20k "   " " . . . . 2 002° "
    18k "   " " . . . . 1 995° "

```
15k will melt at . . . . . . . . . . . 1 992°  "
13k  "    "    "  . . . . . . . . . . . 1 990°  "
12k  "    "    "  . . . . . . . . . . . 1 987°  "
10k  "    "    "  . . . . . . . . . . . 1 982°  "
 9k  "    "    "  . . . . . . . . . . . 1 979°  "
 8k  "    "    "  . . . . . . . . . . . 1 973°  "
 7k  "    "    "  . . . . . . . . . . . 1 960°  "
Pure copper  . . . . . . . . . . . . . 1 994°  "
Fine silver . . . . . . . . . . . . . . 1 873°  "
Composition . . . . . . . . . . . . . 1 587°  "
Pure Spelter . . . . . . . . . . . .    773°   "
```

Table of Weights.

QUALITIES.					OZS.	DWTS.	GRS
24k of given dimensions will weigh					1	0	0
23k "	"	"	"	"		19	12
22k "	"	"	"	"		19	0
20k "	"	"	"	"		18	0
18k "	"	"	"	"		17	12
15k "	"	"	"	"		16	0
13k "	"	"	"	"		15	0
12k "	"	"	"	"		14	12
10k "	"	"	"	"		14	0
9k "	"	"	"	"		13	12
8k "	"	"	"	"		13	0
7k "	"	"	"	"		12	12
Silver	"	"	"	"		10	12
Spelter	"	"	"	"		9	0
Composition	"	"	"	"		8	12
Copper	"	"	"	"		7	12

CHAPTER II.

GOLD SOLDERS.

Solder for 18k gold :

Gold	14 grs.
Silver	6 "
Copper	4 "

For 18k red gold :

Gold	14 grs.
Silver	5 "
Copper	5 "

For 16k gold :

Gold	12 grs.
Silver	7 "
Copper	5 "

For 16k red gold :

Gold	12 grs.
Silver	7 "
Copper	5 "

For 14k gold :

Gold	12 grs.
Silver	8 "
Copper	6 "

For 14k gold :

Gold	1 oz.
Silver	5 dwts.

For 20k gold :

Gold . . . . 1 oz.
Silver . . . . 4 dwts.

For 20k gold :

Gold . . . . 12 dwts.
Silver . . . . 7 "

Pale gold solder :

Alloyed gold . . . . 1 dwt. 6 grs.
Silver . . . . 1 "

For 8k gold :

Gold . . . . 7½ dwts.
Silver . . . . 9 "   18 grs.
Copper . . . . 6 "   18 "
Brass . . . .   15 "

For 5k gold :

Gold . . . . 5 dwts.
Silver . . . . 13 "
Copper . . . . 6 "
Brass . . . . 15 grs.

For 3k gold :

Gold . . . . 1 dwt.
Copper . . . . 1 "
Brass . . . . 1 "
Silver . . . . 4 "

Copper solder :

Coin silver . . . . 16 dwts.
Copper . . . . 3 "
Brass . . . . 1 "

For 10k gold :

14k gold . . . . 10 dwts.
Hard silver solder . . . . . . 22 "

For 6k gold :

    Fine gold . . . . 6 dwts.
    Silver . . . . 12 "
    Copper . . . . 6 "

For 5k gold :

    14k gold . . . . 6 dwts.
    Hard silver solder . . . . : . . 8 "

Metallic Elements.

NAME OF MATAL.	SYMBOL.	SPECIFIC GRAVITY
Platinum	Pt.	21 45
Gold	Au.	19 35
Mercury	Hg.	13 56
Lead	Pb.	11 40
Silver	Ag.	10 48
Bismuth	Bi.	9 84
Copper	Cu.	8 90
Nickel	Ni.	8 55
Iron	Fe.	7 78
Tin	Sn.	7 27
Zinc	Zn.	7 00
Antimony	Sb.	6 75
Arsenic	As.	5 80
Aluminum	Al.	2 58

CHAPTER III.

SILVER ALLOYS.

Cheap silver :

Silver	2 ozs.
Copper	7 dwts.
Brass	7 "
Bismuth	6 "
Salt	6 "
White arsenic	2 "
Potash	2 "

1—Common silver :

Silver	6 ozs.
Copper	4

2—Common silver :

Silver	1 oz.
Copper	10 dwts.

1 - Good silver alloy :

Silver	11 ozs.
Copper	18 dwts.

2—Good silver :

Silver	1 oz.
Copper	1 dwt. 12 grs.

3—Good silver :

Silver	1 oz.
Brass	5 dwts.

1—French silver :
    Silver . . . . 18 dwts.
    Copper . . . . 2 "

2—French silver :
    Silver . . . . 19 dwts.
    Copper . . . . 1 "

SILVER SOLDER.

1—Silver solder, hard :
    Silver . . . . 1 oz.
    Brass . . . . 10 dwts.

2—Silver solder, hard :
    Silver . . . . 1 oz.
    Brass . . . . 10 dwts.
    Spelter . . . . 2 "

3—Silver solder, hard :
    Silver . . . . 14 dwts.
    Copper . . . . 8 "

1—Common silver solder :
    Silver . . . . 16 dwts.
    Copper . . . . 12 grs.
    Brass . . . . 3 dwts. 12 grs.

2—Common silver solder :
    Silver . . . . 10 ozs.
    Brass . . . . 6 " 10 dwts.
    Spelter . . . . 15 dwts.

1—Easy silver solder :
    Silver . . . . 20 ozs.
    Copper . . . . 3 " 8 dwts.
    Brass . . . . 13 "
    Spelter . . . . 1 "

2—Easy silver solder:

    Silver . . . . 13 dwts. 8 grs.
    Brass . . . . 3 "   16 "

3—Easy silver solder:

    Silver . . . . 4 ozs.
    Brass . . . . 22 dwts.
    Zinc . . . . 12 "

4—Easy silver solder:

    Silver . . . . 1 oz
    Brass . . . . 10 dwts.

1—Very common solder:

    Silver . . . . 1 oz.
    Brass . . . . 1 "
    Arsenic (white) . . . . 1 "

2—Very Common solder:

    Silver . . . . 1 oz.
    Brass . . . . 10 dwts.
    Arsenic . . . . 5 "

Medium solder:

    Silver . . . . 1 oz.
    Copper . . . . 3 dwts.
    Arsenic (yellow) . . . . 5 "

Medium silver solder:

    Silver . . . . 15 dwts.
    Copper . . . . 4 "
    Spelter . . . . 1 "

Solder for aluminum:

    Spelter . . . . 18 dwts.
    Aluminum . . . . 1 "   6 grs.
    Copper . . . . 18 grs.

Silver solder for gold plating :
```
Silver . . . . . . . . . . . . 1 oz.
Copper. . . . . . . . . . . . 5 dwts.
Brass . . . . . . . . . . . . 5  "
```

Solder for aluminum :
```
Aluminum . . . . . . . . . . 5 ozs.
Zinc . . . . . . . . . . . . .20  "
```

Best hard solder :
```
Silver . . . . . . . . . . . 16 dwts.
Copper · · . . . . . . . . . 3  "   12 grs.
Spelter . . . . . . . . . . .. . 12 grs.
```

Quick silver solder :
```
Silver . . . . . . . . . . . 10 dwts.
Brass . . . . . . . . . . . . 5  "
Block Tin . . . . . . . . . . 1  "
```

Quick-running solder :
```
Silver . . . . . . . . . . . 1 oz.
Brass . . . . . . . . . . . 10 dwts.
Pure tin . . . . . . . . . . 2  "
```

SOFT SOLDERS.

Bismuth solder :
```
Bismuth . . . . . . . . . . 6 ozs.
Lead . . . . . . . . . . . . 7  "  10 dwts.
Tin . . . . . . . . . . . . .10  "  10  "
```

Soft solder :
```
Lead . . . . . . . . . . . . 1 oz.
Pure tin . . . . . . . . . . 2  "
```

Quick soft solder :
```
Bismuth . . . . . . . . . . 2 ozs.
Tin . . . . . . . . . . . . 1  "
Lead . . . . . . . . . . . . 1  "
```

Fusing Points of Solders.

Haid solder will melt at . . . . 1866° Fahr.
Medium "   "   "   " . . . . 1843°   "
Easy   "   "   "   " . . . . 1818°   "
Common "   "   "   " . . . . 1826°   "
Quick   "   "   "   " . . . . 1802°   "

Fusing Points of Metals.

NAME OF METALS.	FAHR.	CENTI.
Platinum—(infusible except by oxyhydro blowpipe).		
Cast iron	2786°	1530°
Nickel	2700°	1482°
Gold	2016°	1102°
Copper	1994°	1090°
Silver	1873°	1023°
Aluminum	1300°	705°
Zinc	773°	412°
Lead	612°	322°
Bismuth	497°	258°
Tin	442°	228°
Antimony—(fuses below red heat).		
Arsenic—(volatilizes before it fuses).		

CHAPTER IV.

GENERAL ALLOYS.

Imitation gold :

Silver	2 ozs. 5 dwts.
Copper	1 "
Composition	1 "

(Composition for same).

Copper	44 ozs.
Spelter	8 "

Imitation silver :

Silver	1 oz.
Nickel	1 " 11 dwts.
Copper	2 " 9 "

Silverine :

Silver	3 ozs.
Nickel	1 " 11 dwts.
Copper	2 " 9 "
Spelter	10 dwts.

1—Counterfeit gold :

Platina	4 ozs.
Copper	2 " 10 dwts.
Zinc	1 "
Tin	2 "
Lead	1 " 10 "

2—Counterfeit gold :

Platina	1 oz.
Silver	10 dwts.
Copper	1 oz. 10 dwts.

Oreide :

Copper . . . . 4 ozs.
Zinc . . . . 1 " 16 dwts.

Counterfeit silver :

Copper . . . . 1 oz.
Tin . . . . 24 "
Antimony . . . . 1 " 10 dwts.
Bismuth . . . . 5 dwts.

German silver :

Copper . . . . 25 ozs.
Zinc . . . . 15 "
Nickel . . . . 10 "

Gold amalgam :

Gold . . . . 8 dwts.
Mercury . . . . 1 "

Simple oreide :

Copper . . . . 90 ozs.
Zinc . . . . 30 "

Another simple oreide :

Copper . . . . 100 ozs.
Zinc . . . . 50 "

Alloy for compensation balances :

Silver . . . . 2 ozs.
Copper . . . . 2 "
Zinc . . . . 1 "

Artificial gold :

Copper . . . . 100 ozs.
Tin . . . . 17 "

Aluminum alloy :

Copper . . . . 35 ozs.
Nickel . . . . 11 " 10 dwts.
Aluminum . . . . 3 " 10 "

Fictitious silver:

Nickel . . . . 1 oz. 11 dwts.
Copper . . . . 2 " 9 "
Silver . . . . 1 "

Another:

Silver . . . . 1 oz.
Nickel . . . . 1 " 11 dwts
Copper . . . . 2 " 9 "

Malleable brass:

Copper . . . . 33 ozs.
Zinc . . . . 25 "

Babbitt metal:

Copperas . . . . 4 ozs.
Antimony . . . . 3 "
Tin . . . . 96 "

Non-Tarnishable brass:

Zinc . . . . 72 ozs.
Tin . . . . 21 "
Copper . . . . 7 "

White brass:

Copper . . . . 1 oz.
Zinc . . . . 8 "
Iron . . . . 1 "

Japanese brass:

Copper . . . . 10 ozs.
Zinc . . . . 5 "

Common brass:

Copper . . . . 6 ozs.
Zinc . . . . 2 "

Imitation gold :

    Copper . . . . 16 ozs.
    Zinc . . . . 1 "
    Platinum . . . . 7 "

Hard white metal :

    Aluminum . . . . 20 ozs.
    Silver . . . . 1 "

Imitation gold—(non-tarnishable) :

    Copper . . . . 50 ozs.
    Zinc . . . . 25 "

Another :

    Copper . . . . 45 ozs.
    Zinc . . . . 15 "

Imitation silver :

    Silver . . . . 2 ozs. 1 gr.
    Copper . . . . 65 " 10 "
    Zinc . . . . 19 " 10 dwts.
    Nickel . . . . 13 "
    Cobalt and iron . . . . 2 dwts.

Low temperature alloy :

    Bismuth . . . . 47 ozs. 2 dwts.
    Cadmium . . . . 13 " 1 "
    Lead . . . . 19 " 3 " 12 grs.
    Tin . . . . 20 "

Alloy for composition files :

    Copper . . . . 4 ozs.
    Tin . . . . 1 "
    Lead . . . . 10 dwts.
    Zinc . . . . 10 "

Imitation gold :

    Copper . . . . 79 ozs. 17 dwts.
    Zinc . . . . 85 " 1 "
    Nickel . . . . 9 " 2 "

Clark's patent alloy :

Copper	1 oz.	
Spelter	1 dwts.	22 grs.
Cobalt		12 "
Nickel	*3 dwts.	18 "
Tin		12 "

Imitation silver—(non-tarnishable) :

Copper	1 oz.	
Nickel	3 dwts.	12 grs.
Bismuth		6 "
Zinc	2 "	12 "
Soft iron		12 "
Tin		12 "

Alluminum alloy :

Copper	18 dwts.
Aluminum	2 "

CHAPTER V.

HARD ENAMELS.

1—Flux :

    Red lead . . . . 16 ozs.

    Calcined borax . . . . 3 "

    Powdered flint glass . . . . . 12 "

       "   flints . . . . 4 "

After fusing for twelve hours reduce to a powder in a mortar.

II.

    Tin . . . . 3 ozs.

    Lead . . . . 10 "

    Calcine or flux . . . . 4 "

    Pure sand or powdered flint . . 4 "

    Sea salt . . . . 1 "

Partially fuse in a crucible.

III.

    Lead . . . . 4 ozs.

    Tin . . . . 4 "

    Calcine . . . . 1 "

    Flint . . . . 1 "

    Carbonate of Potash . . . . 2 "

       Proceed as above.

IV.

    Flint glass . . . . 3 ozs

    Red Lead . . . . 1 "

       Proceed as before.

V.

    Red lead . . . . 18 ozs.

    Borax (not calcined) . . . . 11 "

    Flint glass . . . . 16 "

       Proceed as before.

VI.

Powdered flint . . . . 10 ozs.

Nitre . . . . 1 "

White arsenic . . . . 1 "

In the above formulae, by increasing the quantity of sand, glass or flux the enamel is rendered more fusible and the opacity and whiteness is increased by the addition of oxide of tin—(*putty powder.*) The use of too much borax is apt to make the enamel effervescent and lose its color.

Black enamel :

Calcined iron . . . . 12 ozs.

Oxide of cobalt . . . . 1 "

White flux . . . . 13 "

Black enamel :

Pure clay . . . . 3 ozs.

Protoxide of iron . . . . . . 1 "

Black enamel :

Peroxide of manganese . . . 3 ozs.

Zaffre . . . . 1 "

Mix and add as required to white flux.

Blue enamel :

White flux . . . . 4 ozs.

Cobalt (oxide) . . . . Enough to color.

Blue enamel :

Sand, ⎫
Red lead, ⎬ . . . . 10 ozs.
Nitre. ⎭

Flint glass . . . . 20 "

Oxide of cobalt . . . . 1 "

Brown enamel :

Manganese . . . . 5 ozs.

Red lead . . . . 16 "

Powdered flint . . . . 8 "

Brown enamel:

Manganese	9 ozs.
Red lead	34 "
Flint powder	16 "

Brown enamel:

Red lead	1 oz.
Calcined iron	1 "
Antimony	2 "
Litharge	2 "
Sand	2 "

Add to required amount of white flux.

Green enamel:

Flux	2 lbs.
Copper (black oxide)	1 oz.

Green enamel:

Flux	2 lbs.
Black oxide copper	1 oz.
Red oxide iron	½ drachm.

Green enamel:

Copper dust	2 ozs.
Litharge	2 "
Nitre	1 "
Sand	4 "

Add flux according to depth of colar required.

Green enamel:

Flux	4 ozs.
Oxide of chromium	Enough to color.

Produces a dead leaf tinge.

Light green enamel:

Flux	5 ozs.
Black oxide of copper	30 grs.
Oxide of chromium	2 "

Green enamel :

    Blue enamel . . . . 2 ozs.
    Yellow . . . . 2 "

Olive enamel :

    Blue enamel . . . . 2 ozs.
    Black   " . . . . 1 "
    Yellow " . . . . 1 "

Orange enamel :

    Red lead . . . . 12 ozs.
    Red sulphate of iron . . . . 1 "
    Oxide of antimony . . . . . 1 "
    Powdered flint . . . . 3 "
    Flux . . . . 50 "
Calcine together the flint before adding the flux.

Orange enamel :

    Red lead . . . . 12 ozs.
    Oxide of antimony . . . . . 4 "
    Powdered flint . . . . 3 "
    Red sulphate of iron . . . . 1 "
    Flux 5 ozs. to every 2 parts of this mixture after calcining.

Purple enamel :

    Flux . . . . 4 ozs.
    Oxide of gold,   } . . Enough to color.
    Peroxide of manganese, }

Red enamel :

    Flux . . . . 4 ozs.
    Red oxide of copper to color.

Red enamel :

    Flux . . . . 4 ozs.
    Color with chloride of gold.

Red enamel :

Sulphate of iron (calcined
dark) . . . . 1 oz.
Flux . . . . 6 "
Colcothar . . . . 3 "

Light red enamel :

Red sulphate of iron . . . . 2 ozs.
Flux . . . . 6 "
White lead . . . . 3 "

Rose enamel :

Purple enamel . . . . 3 ozs.
Flux . . . . 90 "
Oxide of silver . . . . 1 "

Transparent enamel :

Flux without coloring matter.

Violet enamel :

Purple enamel . . . . 2 ozs.
Red enamel . . . . 3 "
Flux . . . . 6 "

Violet enamel :

Saline flux . . . . 4 ozs.
Peroxide of manganese enough to color.

White enamel :

Calcine (from 2 tin and 1 lead.) 1 oz.
Fine crystal glass . . . . . . 2 "
Manganese . . . . 6 grs.
When hot pour into clean water, then powder and fuse again.

Crimson enamel :

Purple cassius . . . . 1 oz.
Flux . . . . 8 "

White enamel :

    Diaphoretic antimony   1 oz.
    Fine glass . . . . 3 "
Mix and proceed as before.

White enamel :

    Lead . . . . 30 ozs.
    Tin . . . . 33 "
    Calcine . . . . 50 "
    Flint powder . . . . 50 "
    Salt of tartar . . . . 100 "

Yellow enamel :

    Flux . . . . 4 ozs.
Fuse with oxide of lead and oxide of iron.

Yellow enamel :

    Lead . . . . 1 oz.
    Tin ashes . . . . 1 "
    Litharge . . . . 1 "
    Antimony . . . . 1 "
    Sand . . . . 1 "
    Nitre . . . . 4 "
Mix, fuse and powder and add flux enough to reduce color.

Yellow enamel :

    White oxide of antimony . . 1 oz.
    Alum . . . . 1 "
    Salammoniac . . . . 1 "
    Pure carbonate of lead . . . 2 "
Fuse to a high enough temperature to fuse the salammoniac.

CHAPTER VI.

ELECTRO-PLATING.

In electro-plating the chief thing is to consider *what battery to use*, as one must be obtained that will give a constant current, and which will not need too frequent changes of solution. The best battery for this purpose is the Daniels battery. The solution for it is cheap, the poles or elements being zinc and copper, the zinc being the minus or negative pole, the copper the plus or positive pole. The article to be plated is always suspended on the wire leading from the zinc pole, and on the other wire leading from the copper is suspended the "anode," gold, silver or nickel, as the case may be. Great care must be exercised to have the work perfectly or *chemically* clean, or failure of the metal to adhere is sure to ensue. The work may be effectively cleaned by dipping into a boiling solution of caustic potash and then rinsed and brushed with bicarbonate of soda or pulverized pumice stone. When the wires or binding screws become corroded or dirty, they must be at once cleaned, for the secret of good results is *cleanliness*. When the battery is not in use remove the elements and cover up the whole to keep it free from dust. It is not absolutely necessary to remove the elements from a Daniels battery. as they will last five or six months if never touched, but when not in use it is well to short circuit the battery, or, in other words, connect the two wires. If using a Bunsen's battery (which is a good one), *always* remove the elements (zinc and carbon), when not in use.

Suppose, for an example, you wish to plate a piece of brass or copper work. First dip it into the solution of potash, remove and rinse with hot water and brush with damp bicarbonate of soda, or, if to be positive of a perfect result, after using the potash you may dip into a solution composed of

Sulphuric acid	1 drop.
Nitric acid	25 ozs.
Salt	1 "

Remove and rinse, then dip again into a solution of

Nitrate of mercury	1 oz.
Sulphuric acid	½ "
Water	100 "

which will coat the article with a very thin film of mercury, to which the plate will readily adhere. Next suspend the article on the wire leading from the zinc of the battery and let it hang in the bath, then immerse your piece of pure silver or gold, being suspended from the wire leading from the copper of the battery, care being taken not to let the wires touch one another and to keep the anode about ten or twelve inches away from the articles to be plated. Proceed at once to set the battery in action, and if the solution is in good order the plating will at once begin. If it is a silver solution, the article will become a bluish-white color; if of gold the color will be a dull yellow. For silver allow it to remain in the bath about twenty or thirty minutes, for gold a little less. It should then be removed and well washed in water, then scratch brushed with a fine brass wire brush or burnished with soapy water, as may be desired. If the plate should not be thick enough to stand these operations it may be put back into the bath and allowed to stand for another twenty minutes or thereabouts before scratch brushing or burnishing. A moderate amount of solution for general work is about one gallon, which should be used in a glass, wood or porcelain vessel. The anode employed would be about $2x4x\frac{1}{16}$ inches. If the solution is not in good order, after being used only a few times it may be well filtered and allowed to stand twenty-four hours before using again. The scratch brush should revolve at a high speed, and a little stale beer should be used to keep the article wet. Care should be taken to keep the article clear from finger marks, both before and after plating. Bloodstone burnishers are preferable to steel ones, as they are much smoother and not so liable to strip the plating off.

PLATING BATHS—SILVER.

Silver plating solution :

        Cyanide of potasium . . . . 6 ozs.
        Nitrate of silver . . . . . . 1 "
        Distilled water . . . . 32 "
Use with weak battery.

Silver plating solution :

Nitrate of silver . . . . . . 1 oz.
Cyanide of potasium . . . . 2 "
Distilled water . . . . 12 "

Use without battery.

Silver plating powder :

Chloride of silver . . . . . 3 ozs.
Cream of tartar (pulverized) . 20 "
Cooking salt . . . . 15 "

Mix well and rub on surface to be plated, with a soft cloth.

Silver plating fluid :

Nitrate of silver . . . . . . 2 ozs.
Distilled water . . . . 14 "
Cyanide of potassium . . . . 4 "

Use without battery.

Silver plating solution :

Nitrate of silver . . . . . . 1 oz.
Salt . . . . 1 "
Cyanide of potasium . . . . 1 " 2½ dwts.
Distilled water . . . . 32 "

Use with battery after 24 hours' standing.

Silver plating fluid :

Nitrate silver . . . . 1 oz.
Cyanide of potassium . . . . 2 "
Spanish whiting . . . . . . 4 "
Rain water . . . . 10 "

Apply with soft brush and finish with chamois skin or burnisher.

Silver plating powder :

Nitrate of silver . . . . . . 15 grs.
Tartar . . . . 2 drachms.
Salt . . . . 2 "
Powdered alum . . . . . . ½ "

Use as above.

Silver plating solution :

     Nitrate of silver . . . . . . ½ oz.
     Cyanide of potassium . . . . 8 "
     Distilled water . . . . 32 "
Use with strong battery.

Quick-plating silver solution :

     Nitrate of silver . . . . . . 1 oz.
     Distilled water . . . . 20 "

Add enough solution of salammoniac to form a precipitate ; then filter and wash the precipitate ; then add 5 dwts. sulphate of soda mixed with lime water, then paint article with a brush and rinse in in water.

Silvering powder :

     Chloride of silver . .   1 oz.
     Pearl ashes . . . . 3 "
     Salt . . . . 1½ "
     Whiting . . . . 1 "

Mix together and apply with a chamois skin.

Silver plating iron :

     Nitrate of silver . . . . . . 1 oz.
     Cyanide of potassium . . . . 2 "
     Sulphate of soda . . . . . . ½ "
     Distilled water . . . . 12 "

Use without battery after brass plating the article with following bath: (First clean in diluted sulphuric acid). Sulphate of zinc, 1 oz.; sulphate of copper, 2 ozs.; cyanide of potassium, 3 ozs.; distilled water, 12 ozs.

Silver powder for copper :

     Chloride of silver . . . . . 4 ozs.
     Cream of tartar . . . . 4 "
     Alum . . . . 2 ,,

. Mix with water to a paste and apply with chamois skin.

Silver plating solution :

    Nitrate of silver . . . . . . 1 oz.
    Cyanide of potassium . . . . 4 "
    Distilled water . . . . 1 gal.

Dissolve the nitrate of silver in one quart of water, then pour in it
a saturated solution of salt, which will immediately precipitate the
silver. Keep on adding the salt until the silver ceases falling, then
pour off the fluid, leaving the silver in the bowl. Then wash the
salt off the silver and add four ounces of cyanide of potassium to it
(the silver), well mix and put in enough water to make one gallon
of plating fluid. Finish by filteringthe whole. Use cold with strong
battery.

GOLD PLATING SOLUTIONS.

I.

    Chloride of gold . . . . . . 2 dwts.
    Cyanide of Potassium . . . . 2 ozs. 12 pwts.
    Distilled water . . . . 64 "
Use hot with weak battery and 24k anode.

II.

    Chloride of gold . . . . . . 5 dwts.
    Cyanide of potassium . . . . 1 oz. 2½ dwts.
    Rain water . . . . 32 "
Use hot with battery and gold anode.

Red gold plating :   III.

    Cyanide of Potassium . . . . 1 oz.
    Chloride of gold . . . . . . 15 grs.
    Sulphate of coppor . . . . . 5 dwts.
    Distilled water . . . . 40 ozs.
Filter the whole well after dissolving and use hot with battery and
gold anode.

IV.

Distilled water . . . . 4 ozs.
Chloride of gold . . . . . . 15 grs.
Carbonate of magnesia . . . 1 "
Tincture of cucuma . . . 50 drops.
Cyanide of potassium . . . . ¼ oz.

Use while hot; for a deeper color add sulphate of copper one-half grain and tincture of cucuma five drops to every ounce of solution. Suspend the article on a clean zinc strip.

Gold plating fluid :   V.

Distilled water . . . . 3 ozs.
Alcohol . . . . 2 "
Aqua ammonia . . . . 1 "
Sulphate of soda . . . . . . ¼ "
"   " copper . . . . ⅛ "
Chloride of gold . . . . . . 4 grs.

Use while hot, with zinc as above.

VI.

Crystallized phosphate of
soda . . . . 60 ozs.
Bisulphide of soda . . . . . 1 "
Cyanide of potassium . . . . 1 "
Chloride of gold . . . . . . 2½ dwts.
Distilled water . . . . 1000 ozs.

Divide water into three parts—one of 700 and two of 150. Disolve sodic phosphate in the first portion, chloride of gold in second, bisulphide of soda and cyanide in the third. Use with weak battery and platinum anode.

VII.

Distilled water . . . . 64 ozs.
Cyanide of potassium . . . . 5 "
Chloride of gold . . . . . . 1 dwt.

Use warm with battery and gold anode.

VIII.

To gild small steel articles :

      Chloride of gold . . . . . . 2 dwts.
      Sulphuric ether . . . . . . 3 ozs.

Allow to stand in corked bottle for twenty four hours, then clean article and drip.

Gold plating powder :

      Chloride of gold . . . . . . 5 dwts.
      Cyanide of potassium . . . . 2 ozs.
      Rain water . . . . 16 "
      Spanish Whiting . . . . . . 1 lb.

Let the whole evaporate in open air till dry.

Electro-brass-plating.

      Sodium bicarbonate . . . . 42 grs.
      Ammonium chloride . . . . 27 "
      Cyanide of potassium . . . 6½ "
      Distilled water . . . . . . 32 ozs.

From each wire of battery attach a piece of cast brass, and allow the current to run for one hour and remove the brass attached t⁰ zinc pole and replace with article to be plated.

To copper plate steel :

      Sulphate of copper . . . . . 9 grs.
      Chloride of tin . . . . . . 9 "
      Water . . . . 28 ozs.

Use without battery.

Copper plating :

      Sulphate of copper . . . . . 4 ozs.
      Sulphuric acid . . . . 1 "
      Distilled water . . . . . . 12 ozs.

Dissolve the sulphate of copper in 8 ozs. of boiling water. When cold, add the sulphuric acid and remainder of water. Use cold with battery.

Copper plating :

Dissolve 1 lb. of sulphate of copper in 2 quarts boiling water. When cold add ¼ its bulk of sulphuric acid, dissolved in proportion of 1 lb. to 5 pints of water. Use as preceding.

NICKEL PLATING SOLUTIONS.

I.

Chloride of sinc . . . . . . 1½ ozs.
Distilled water . . . . 100 "

Add enough sulphate of nickel to turn the solution green. Use while hot and suspend article on a wire for half an hour.

II.

Sulphate of nickel . . . . . 10 ozs.
Distilled water . . . . 128 "
Ammonia . . . . 5 "

Use with weak battery with nickel anode.

III.

Granulated tin . . . . 1 oz.
Tartar . . . . ½ "
Distilled water . . . . 16 "

Heat till boiling, add ½ oz. of pure red-hot oxide of nickel. For copper and brass only.

IV.

Sulphate of nickel . . . . 2 ozs.
Distilled water . . . . 2 quarts.

Boil together ; when cold filter and use with strong battery.

CHAPTER VII.

CEMENTS.

Fine cement—(impervious to acids.)

Pulverized oxide of lead . . 1 oz.
Glycerine . . . . 1 "

Cement for porcelain :

Fresh cheese . . . . 2 ozs.
Silicate of potassium . . . . 1 "
Apply immediately.

Strong liquid cement :

Rice (pulverized) . . . . . . 4 ozs.
Water . . . . 6 "
Mix together cold, add boiling water, then boil for five minutes.

Glass cement :

Rubber . . . . 1 oz
Mastic . . . . 3 "
Chloroform . . . . 5 "
Dissolve for three days and then apply, and keep air tight all the time. Dries quickly.

Shellac cement :

Shellac . . . . 1 oz.
Alcohol . . . . 2 "

Celluloid cement :

Shellac . . . . 1 oz.
Spirits of camphor . . . . . 1 "
Alcohol . . . . 4 "
Apply warm.

Jeweler's cement :

Isinglass . . . . 2 ozs.
Gum Arabic . . . . 1 "
Alcohol . . . . 1 "

Cork loosely and boil in a vessel of hot water. Then strain for use.

Lathe cements :

Shellac . . . . 8 ozs.
Ultramarine (blue) . . . . . ½ "

Common cement :

Resin . . . . 4 ozs.
Brick dust . . . . 4 "

Common black cement :

Resin . . . . 2 ozs.
Brick dust . . . . 2 "
Lamp black . . . . 2 "

Second-hand-dial cement :

Plaster of Paris (pulverized . 4 ozs.
White glue . . . . 3 "

Hardens in 24 hours.

Transparent cement—(diamond.)

Chloroform . . . . 12 drachms.
Caoutchouc (non-vulcanized.).12½ "
Mastic . . . . 2½ "

Allow to stand nine days, shaking continually.

Metal cement :

Caustic soda . . . . 1 oz.
Resin . . . . 3 "
Water . . . . 5 "
Plaster of Paris . . . . . . 4½ "

Hardens in thirty minutes.

Metal cement:

```
            Litharge . . . . . . . . . .  2 ozs.
            White lead . . . . . . . .   1  "
            Boiled linseed oil . . . . . .  3  "
            Gum copal . . . . . . . .    1  "
Use immediately.
```

Common engraver's cement :

```
            Pitch . . . . . . . . . . .  4 ozs.
            Resin . . . . . . . . . . .  4  "
            Shellac . . . . . . . . . .  1  "
```

Rubber cement :

```
            Shellac (pulverized) . . . .  1 oz.
            Spirits of ammonia . . . . 10  "
Ready for use after three days.
```

Impervious cement:

```
            Litharge . . . . . . . . . .  5 ozs.
            White sand . . . . . . .     3  "
            Plaster of Paris . . . . . .  3  "
            Resin (pulverized) . . . . .  1  "
Boiled linseed oil (with driers) enough to make a paste.   Use after
five hours.   Keep air tight.
```

Acid-proof cement :

```
            Rubber . . . . . . . . . .  2 ozs.
            Linseed oil . . . . . . . .  4  "
Add enough white bolus to make up a consistency.
```

Fire proof cement :

```
            Pulverized asbestos . . . .  2 ozs.
            Waterglass . . . . . . . . .  2  "
Mix well.
```

1—Alabaster cement :

Dip broken edges into melted alum and join together quickly.

2—Alabaster cement :

Yellow resin, } Melt together 2 ozs. each.
Beeswax,

Gypsum . . . . 2 ozs.

Amber cement :

Gum Arbaic (liquid) . . . . . 1 oz.
Plaster of Paris . . . . 1½ "

Use at once and let article stand for 12 hours.

Watch glass cement :

Gum Arabic . . . . 3½ ozs.
Crystallized sugar . . . . . 1½ "
Distilled water . . . . 2 "

Dissolve by gently heating.

Engraver's cement :

Beeswax . . . . 2 ozs.
Pitch . . . . 4 "
Tallow . . . . 2 "

Silver and gold-colored cement :

Shellac . . . . 10 ozs.
Venetian turpentine . . . . 3⅓ "
Bronze (gold or silver) . . . . 1 "

First melt shellac and then add the remainder.

Colorless cement :

Isinglass . . . . 2 ozs.
Alcohol . . . . 2 "
Gum ammonia . . . . 10 grs.
Gum mastic . . . . 6 drops.

Soften the isinglass with water first.

Chaser's cement :

Pitch . . . . 4 ozs.
Resin . . . . 4 "
Brick dust . . . . 2 "

Engravers, cement :

Pitch . . . . 4 ozs.
Resin . . . . 4 "
Plaster of Paris . . . . 2 "
Beeswax . . . . 2 "

CHAPTER VIII.

PICKLES, SOLDERING SOLUTIONS, ETC.

Silver pickle :

Sulphuric acid . . . . 1 oz.
Water . . . . 10 "

Use boiling in copper pan.

Gold pickle :

Nitric acid . . . . 1 oz.
Water . . . . 8 "

Use boiling as above.

Pickle for tarnish :

Cyanide of potassium . . . . 1 oz.
Water . . . . 8 "

Pickle for brass :

Oxalic acid . . . . 1 oz.
Water . . . . 3 "

Strong cleaning pickle :

Sulphuric acid . . . . 2 ozs.
Nitric acid . . . . 1 "
Water . . . . 8 "

Use while hot.

Pickle to remove dirt :

Nitric acid . . . . 10 ozs.
Sulphuric acid . . . . 2 "
Salt . . . . 1 "

Boil and dip articles quickly, then rinse well.

Brass pickle:
Sulphuric acid . . . . ½ oz.
Nitric acid . . . . 1 "
Dip article and rinse well.

Soft soldering fluid:
Muriatic acid . . . . 3 ozs.
Zinc . . . . 1 "

Non-corrosive soldering fluid:
Muriatic acid . . . . 2 ozs.
Zinc . . . . ½ "
Spirits of ammonia . . . . . ¾ "
Rain water . . . . 2½ "

Soft soldering fluid:
Muriatic acid . . . . 3 ozs.
Zinc . . . . 1½ "
Salammoniac . . . . 60 "
Rain water . . . . 1½ "

Non-corrosive soldering fluid:
Lactic acid . . . . 1 oz.
Glycerine . . . . 1 "
Water . . . . 8 "

Non-corrosive soldering fluid:
Chloride of zinc . . . . . . 1 oz.
Alcohol . . . . 3 "

Pickle to remove blue from steel:
Muriatic acid . . . . 4 ozs.
Elixir vitriol . . . . 4 "

Pickle for removing grease:
Potash . . . . 1 ℔.
Water . . . . 2 gal.
Spirits of ammonia . . . . . 2 ozs.
Use boiling.

Pickle to remove tarnish :
Cyanide of potassium . . . . 1 oz.
Rain water . . . . 1 pint.

Pickle to remove soft solder :
Spirits of salts.

Pickle to remove enamel :
Fluor spar (pulverized) . . . 3 ozs.
Sulphuric acid . . . . 5 "
Boil the article.

Hard soldering solution :
Borax . . . . 1 oz.
Alcohol . . . . 4 "

Pickle for frosting :
Salt . . . . ½ oz.
Saltpetre . . . . 4 "
Sulphuric acid . . . . 8 "
Coarseness of frosting depends on quantity of salt.

Brass cleaning pickle :
Sulphuric acid . . . . 2 ozs.
Nitre . . . . 1½ "
Saltpetre . . . . 1 drachm.
Rain water . . . . 2 ozs.

Pickle for frosting silver :
Sulphuric acid . . . . 1 drachm.
Rain water . . . . 4 ozs.
Heat the solution and immerse until frosted as desired.

Pickle for tinging silver like gold :
Sulphuric acid . . . . 1 oz.
Water . . . . 20 "
Iron rust . . . . 3 "
Steep until article is colored.

Pickle to polish brass :

Sulphuric acid . . . . 2 ozs.
Bicromate of potash . . . . 1 "
Distilled water . . . . 3 "

Dip, rinse and polish with rotten stone.

To remove tarnish from gilding :

Common alum . . . . 2 ozs.
Soft water . . . . 6 "

Dip, remove, rinse and dry in sawdust.

Pickle to frost watch plates :

Nitric acid . . . . 2½ ozs.
Muriatic acid . . . . 2 "

Dip quickly, rinse and scratch brush.

To restore pearls.

Caustic potash . . . . 2 ozs.
Water . . . . 5 "
Chalk enough to form a paste.

Place the pearls in a muslin bag and suspend into the warm paste.

Pickle to clean metal dials.

Cyanide of potassium . . . . 1 oz.
Rain water (hot) . . . . . . 32 "
Ammonia . . . . 2 "
Alcohol . . . . ½ "

Dip article and rinse in hot water. Then wash with soap and water, and dry in hot sawdust.

Pickle to restore nickel movements :

Alcohol . . . . 25 ozs.
Sulphuric acid . . . . ½ "
Nitric acid . . . . ½ "

Dip for ten seconds, remove and rinse in cold water, afterwards dip in alcohol and dry.

Pickle to remove oxydize:

    Sulphuric acid . . . . 1 oz.
    Water . . . . 30 "

Anneal the work and boil.

Pickle to remove oxydize:

    Sulphuric acid . . . . 5 ozs.
    Nitric acid . . . . 2½ "
    Muriatic acid . . . . 2 drachms.
    Water . . . . 5 "

Use cold and immerse for a few second.

Pickle to strip silver plate:

I.

    Sulphuric acid . . . . 3 ozs.
    Nitric acid . . . . ½ "

Boil the mixture in crucible and dip the articles in perfectly dry and keep withdrawing, etc., to ascertain the progress made.

II.

    Sulphuric acid . . . . 8 ozs.
    Saltpetre . . . . 2 "

Heat the acid and add the saltpetre, and suspend the work for a short time. If not active enough, keep adding small pieces of saltpetre until the desired effect is obtained.

PICKLES FOR DISSOLVING METALS.

Silver:

    Nitric acid . . . . 4 ozs.
    Water . . . . 2 "

Silver alloys:

    Nitric acid . . . . 2 ozs.
    Water . . . . 4 "

Silver solder:

    Nitric acid . . . . 2 ozs.
    Water . . . . 8 "

Copper :

    Nitric acid . . . . 2 ozs.
    Water . . . . 8 "

Soft solder :

    Perchloride of iron . . . . . 2 ozs.
    Water . . . . 8 "

To dissolve soft solder :

    Protosulphate of iron . . . . 2 ozs.
    Nitrate of potassium . . . . 1 "
    Water . . . . 10 "

Boil in iron dish and let cool, and remove the crystals which appear. Then dissolve them in muriatic acid. (1 oz. crystal to 1 oz. acid). Then add 4 ozs. water and heat with gas, and keep work in while hot.

CHAPTER IX.

OXYDIZES AND COLORINGS.

I.

Oxydes for silver—slate color :

Sulphuret of potassium . . .   2 oz.
Water . . . . .16 "
Salammoniac . . . . . . .⅛ "
Immerse work while boiling.

II.

Sulphate of copper . . . . .   I oz.
Salammoniac . . . . 2 "
Vinegar . . . . 6 "
Use warm.

III.—(Black.)

Sulphate of sodium   . . . . 1 oz.
Water . . . . 6 "
Use hot.

IV.—(For plated goods.)

Salammoniac . . . . 2 ozs.
Sulphate of copper . . . . . 2 "
Saltpetre . . . . 1 "
Acetic acid (*vinegar*) . . . .10 "
Use hot.

V.—(Brown.)

Salammoniac . . . . 2 ozs.
Blue vitriol . . . . 2 "
Vinegar . . . . 8 "

Anti-oxydizer :

Borax	. . . .	2 ozs.
Yellow ochre	. . . .	1 "

Boil together with water.

Anti-oxydize :

Yellow ochre	. . . .	4 ozs.
Boracic acid	. . . .	1 "

Well mix with boiling water and boil for one hour. Use cold with brush.

Violet oxydize for brass :

Chloride of antimony	. . .	2 ozs.
Distilled water	. . . .	6 "

Clean the article with bicarbonate of soda, heat it gently and immerse in the solution.

1—Black oxydize for brass :

Sulphurized natron	. . . .	1 oz.
Copper vitriol	. . . .	2 "
Water (pure)	. . . .	100 "

Use hot.

2—Black oxydize for brass :

Sulphurized natron	. . . . .	1 oz.
Copper vitriol	. . . .	3½ "
Water	. . . .	100 "

Use hot.

3—Dark, for brass :

Sulphurized natron	. . . .	2 ozs.
Sulphuret of potassium	. . .	1 "
Copper vitriol	. . . .	3 "
Water	. . . .	100 "

Use hot.

Oxydize for silver :

Sulphuret of ammonia	. . .	1 oz.
Hot water	. . . .	1 pint.

Oxydize for silver without immersing:

Chloride of platinum . . . . 1 oz.
Sulphuric ether . . . . . . 2 ozs.

Apply with camel hair brush.

Black oxydize for silver:

Saltpetre . . . . 2 ozs.
Salt . . . . 1 "
Muriatic acid . . . . 1 "

Use with brush.

Blue oxydize for silver:

Burn a piece of sulphur in a porcelain vessel and suspend the article, after well polishing, over the fumes. The parts not to be oxidized are to be coated with a resist varnish. During the process keep the fumes covered up.

Bright black oxydize for silver:

Bromine . . . . 5 grs.
Bromide of potassium . . . 5 dwts.
Water . . . . 10 ozs.

Use hot in porcelain vessel and polish with rouge after oxydizing to required color.

Color for nickle and copper:

Lead acetate . . . . 300 grs.
Hyposulphite of soda . . . . 600 "
Water . . . . 32 ozs.

Dissolve first, then boil. The article will change (if copper) eleven different colors, from gray to blue, according to the number of times it is dipped in the solution. Nickle takes 8 colors.

Color for Etruscan gold work.—For 6 ozs. of work.

Saltpetre . . . . 8 ozs.
Salt . . . . 8 "
Muriatic acid . . . . 6 "
Rain water . . . . 2 "

Mix well the saltpetre and water and when hot add the acid. Suspend article on a silver wire and immerse for three minutes, then take them out and rinse well. If necessary, immerse again for half a minute and rinse. Articles to be annealed black before coloring.

American color:

Saltpetre	8 ozs.
Salt	4 "
Muriatic acid	2 "
Salammoniac	4 "
Rain water	2 "

Proceed as above.

Bronze color for any metal:

Aniline red	10 ozs.
" purple	5 "
Alcohol (95 per ct.)	100 "

Warm carefully and add 5 ozs. bronzoic acid, boil well and apply with brush.

To color brass gray:

Carbonate of copper	2 ozs.
Ammonia (liquid)	6 "

Clean article and immerse in the solution.

To color marble:

Blue—Solution of blue litmus.
Yellow—Tincture of gamboge.
Red—Dragon's blood (alkanet.)
Crimson—Alkanet and turpentine.
Pink—Wax with turpentine.
Brown—Tincture of logwood.
Gold—Verdigris, 1 oz.; Salammoniac, 1 oz.; sulphate of zinc, 1 oz. Reduce to powder.

Gold color for brass:

Caustic soda	2 ozs.
Milk sugar	2 "
Distilled water	50 "
Sulphate of copper (solution).	2 "

Boil the first three for 15 minutes, then add sulphate of copper, constantly stirring. Use very hot, though not boiling.

To color aluminum :

Hydrofluoric acid . . . . . 1 oz.
Aqua fortis . . . . 1 "
Rain water . . . . 12 "

Drip the article a short time.

Lacquer for brass :

Sandarac . . . . 6 ozs.
Mastic . . . . 3 "
Elemi . . . . 1 "
Venetian turpentine . . . . ½ "
Alcohol . . . . 32 "

Clean the article well and warm it.

Lacquer for silverware :

Alcohol . . . . 10 ozs.
Collodion . . . . 4 "

Paint with a fine brush and it will dry at once. It can, if necessary, be removed with hot water.

To color clock hands red :

Carmine . . . . 1 oz.
Chloride of silver . . . . . 1 "
Tinners' japan . . . . . . ½ "

Use warm. Apply this to the hands and place them on a copper plate, face up, and gently heat.

To black clock hands :

Paint them with a fine brush with asphaltum varnish.

Lacquer for brass :

Gamboge . . . . 2 ozs.
Shellac . . . . 2 "
Alcohol . . . . 8 "

Color to suit with alkanet.

Blue coating for steel :

. Dip in a solution of nitrate of potash.

To blacken steel or iron:

Sulphur . . . . 1 oz.
Oil of turpentine . . . . . . 10 "

Boil together and apply to metal, then heat the metal until it turns a fine black.

To bronze metals:

Pulverized verdigris . . . . 500 grs.
" salammoniac . . 475 "
Strong vinegar . . . . 160 "
Water . . . . 2 liters.

Boil in a copper vessel and remove with wooden spoon.

To copper coat soft solder:

Nitric acid . . . . ½ oz.
Water . . . . 1 "
Copper . . . . ½ "

When copper has dissolved, the solution is ready for use. Apply with a brush and touch article with a steel wire.

II.

Sulphate of copper (pulverized) . . . . 1 oz.
Water . . . . 6 "

Treat as above.

CHAPTER X.

MISCELLANEOUS.

Powder for cleaning silverware :

        Rouge . . . . 1 oz.
        Prepared chalk . . . . 1 "
Mix well. Use dry with chamois leather.

Powder for cleaning silver and gold :

        Rock alum (pulverized) . . . 5 ozs.
        Powdered chalk . . . . . . 1 "
Mix and apply with a dry brush.

Solution for cleaning silverware :

        Hyposulphate of soda . . . . 2 ozs.
        Water . . . . 3 "
Use with a soft cloth.

To clean files :

        Brush well with benzole.

To clean precious stones :

        Precipitated sulphur . . . . 1 oz.
        Spirits of wine . . . . ¼ "
Rub with solt cloth.

To harden steel tools :

Heat the article to a white heat and thrust into sealing wax. Then withdraw and repeat the operation until cold. Excellent for gravers and drills.

To mark name on tools :

Cover the steel with a thin layer of wax and scratch name through the wax. Then cover with nitric acid and allow to remain a few minutes, rinse in water and remove the wax.

To remove acids from cloths:
Dampen with concentrated spirits of ammonia.

Burnishing powder:

Prepared chalk	4 ozs.
Pipe clay	1 "
White lead	1 "
Carbonate of magnesia	¼ "
Rouge	6 "

To clean brushes:
Wash in a solution of strong soda, rinse well and let dry.

To make a grindstone more effective:
Apply some common carbolic acid.

To clean gypsum figures:

Caustic potash	3 ozs.
Hot water	36 "
Steric acid	9 "

Mix together and dissolve in

Water	21 "
Alcohol	21 "

To brighten dull gold:

Calcium hypochloride	80 grs.
Sodium bicarbonate	80 "
Sodium chloride	20 "
Distilled water	3 quarts.

Immerse article and rinse in water.

To glaze dials:

White shellac (bleached)	½ oz.
Alcohol	4 "

To glaze steel blue:

Damar varnish	8 ozs.
Prussian blue	½ drachm.

To clean gilt articles :

```
Chloride of lime . . . . . . 3⅓ dwts.
Bicarbonate of soda . . . . 3⅓  "
Salt  . . . . . . . . . . .   1  "
```

To clean movements :

Remove all screws and other steel parts. Then immerse in a weak solution of oxalic acid and water, withdraw and then immerse in a cyanide pickle, rinse and dry in sawdust.

To clean nickel plates :

Wash the plates with soap and water, then immerse in a cyanide pickle, rinse and dry in sawdust.

To make prepared chalk :

Powdered chalk, 2 lbs., rain water, 1 gal. Stir well and let stand three minutes, then pour off the water into another vessel and let settle again. This will be prepared chalk after it is thoroughly dried.

To whiten silver :

Anneal the article and let it grow cold, then allow it to stand for one hour in a pickle composed of ten drops of sulphuric acid to two ozs. water.

To make diamantine:

```
Boric acid . . . . . . . . . 25 ozs.
Aluminum  . . . . . . . . . 20  "
```
Melt together until crystallized.

To flatten hair spings :

Remove the collet and stud, then place the spring between two copper surfaces about the size of a cent, then put the whole on a blueing pan, and also lay by its side a small piece of polished steel, then heat, and when the steel turns blue the work is done.

To pivot staffs and pinions:

Drill into the end of the staff or pinion, then insert a piece of steel to fit, turn it down to the desired diameter and polish with bell-metal and oilstone powder. Finish with boxwood and lime.

To drill hard steel.

Make the drill oval in form, then temper as hard as possible. Roughen the surface to be drilled with nitric acid and then drill. When drilling ceases roughen again with nitric acid. Use turpentine as a lubricator.

To polish steel flat :

Roller tables, collets, etc., are rubbed on glass plates with fine emery and oil, then finish on a zinc block with diamantine and alcohol.

To lengthen ancre escapement levers :

Cut across with a screwhead file just back of the fork as deep as possible without injury. A thin point is then left standing, which is then gently bent forward the required distance. This is the quickest process of bringing the point of the lever closer to the roller.

To replace teeth in wheels :

Drill down the plate of the wheel where the old tooth was formerly placed, then tap the hole and screw in a piece of threaded wire, with a shoulder on it like a screw, shape the tooth to match the remainder of teeth.

Oil for stones :

Glycerine . . . . 3 ozs.
Alcohol . . . . 1 "

To polish steel :

Rub article on glass with oilstone powder and oil. Next rub on glass and diamantine and a little oil. Finish on boxwood with lime and alcohol.

To lessen diameter of watch glass :

Place on a marble slab a piece of fine emery paper and rub down the glass on its surface, keeping it continually revolving. After having reduced it, rub on the plain marble, with rottenstone. Then finish with oxide of tin with alcohol.

To fasten ruby pins :

Use asphaltum varnish instead of shellac. It is not so brittle as shellac, though infinitely stronger. Dries in a few minutes.

Soldering set-rings:

Wrap the ring in wet tissue paper, leaving the broken place exposed, and solder quickly.

Diamond test :

When looking through a stone at a needle point hole in a card, if it appears double it is not genuine, as imitation diamonds or colorless stones refract double.

To clean oil stones :

Let it soak for two days in benzine until all the old oil is soaked out, then use with pure glycerine and alcohol.

To fasten roller jewels :

Place jewel in the hole with a small grain of shellac, warm very gently, and the roller is then secured.

To anneal polished steel and save its polish:

Cover the article with grease from the oilstone and anneal with a blowpipe, then clean with benzine.

To bend tempered steel.

Hold in two pairs of pliers over an alcohol flame, and bend as it is turning a straw color.

To write in silver :

    Pewter or tin . . . . 1 oz.
    Mercury . . . . 2 ozs.
Mix with gum water and then write with quill pen.

To whiten silver dials :

Anneal in a copper pan and boil it out in a weak sulphuric pickle, rinse well and dry in sawdust.

To temper drills :

Heat to a cherry red and no higher, then thrust into mercury.

To test the fineness of jewels :

Lay the jewel on charcoal and heat to a cherry red. If the jewel is not perfect and of the correct .density, impurities will appear, which may be seen by the aid of the lens.

To bleach ivory white :

Place the article under a glass cover, wherein is placed a mixture of chloride of lime, 2 ozs., and muriatic acid, 1 oz. Don't inhale the vapor, as it is poisonous. This will restore it to original color.

To blue screws :

Secure an old watch barrel and drill it full of holes ; fill it with brass or copper filings, then replace the cap of barrel, place in the screws from the outside, leaving the heads exposed. Heat the whole over an alcohol flame until the required color is obtained.

To clean clocks :

Remove the escapement, place in a deep dish with enough gasoline to cover the movement, then wind and let run down two or three times, wash the escapement and replace. Let it well dry after rinsing in water 1 pint, alcohol 2 ozs., then oil with good clock oil.

To close a seam in coral :

Heat the article gently and apply watch oil to the crack. It will then be closed when cold.

To tinge soft solder :

Prepare a heavy solution of sulphate of copper and apply with a pencil to soldered spot. Then touch it with an iron wire and it will become coppered. If a yellow color is desired add to the above solution sulphate of zinc.

To demagnetize small steel articles :

Cement article to a small wooden chuck fastened in a lathe and revolve rapidly, hold a magnet within half an inch and draw it away gradually to about fifteen inches and the work is done.

To remove cement :

Place the article in naptha and let remain for twenty minutes, or place in warm turpentine.

To remove temper without spoiling polish :

Enclose articles in a brass cylinder of convenient size with a close-fitting plug, previously filled with brass filings. Heat to cherry red and let it cool gradually.

To drill enamel dials :

Drill with hard drill moistened with turpentine and camphor.

Ivory etching :

Cover the ivory with thin coating of beeswax, then trace the desired figure on the wax and pour over this a strong solution of nitrate of silver. Let it remain a few minutes in a good light, then wash with warm water.

To grind watch plates :

After roughening the surface of a piece of glass on a grindstone, use fine emery with soap while grinding the plates down on it.

Staff measuring :

Remove both end-stones, replace the cock securely, then with a degree gauge, measure from the outside of one hole-jewel to that of the other, and to this add the necessary end-shake. This will be correct measurement.

To test silver :

File the article a little to remove the surface and apply nitric acid. If it boils green and after washing off leaves a gray mark it is silver. If, on the contrary, it leaves a bright mark it is not silver.

Test for gold :

Mix 1 oz. of C. P. nitric acid with two drops of muriatic acid, which will discolor anything under 16 karat gold

To polish jewel settings :

First use a piece of ground glass with rottenstone and oil, finish on boxwood with diamantine and alcohol.

To keep rust off hairsprings :

Paint the paper parcel on the outside with very little olive oil.

To make plating adhere:

First clean in caustic potash and rinse, then in a solution of sulphuric acid, 1 drop, nitric acid, 25 ozs., common salt, 1 oz. Remove and rinse and dip in a solution of nitrate of mercury, 1 oz., water, 100 ozs., sulphuric acid, ½ oz.

To prevent steel rusting:

Melt a small quantity of white wax in benzine and paint with a camel hair brush.

To remove name from dials:

With a copper burnisher use diamond dust and oil. When name is erased polish with more oil and less diamond dust.

To remove rust from pinions:

Scour with oilstone, powder and oil, then polish with crocus and alcohol on a piece of pegwood.

To remove rust from steel pieces:

Use fine emery and oil or fine emery paper and oil and finish with lime and boxwood.

To remove stains from dials:

Apply nitric acid with tissue paper, being careful to wash thoroughly afterwards.

To make ivory flexible:

Immerse in a solution of phosphoric acid (1.13) until it loses its opacity. Rinse in cold water.

To solder stay-springs:

Fasten to a piece of charcoal and use plenty of borax, then proceed to solder with a piece of brass, silver or 18k gold. After soldering temper in the usual manner.

To clean watch movements:

Wash the movement in soapy water, then dip in a cyanide pickle, rinse and dry in sawdust.

To weaken a hair spring:

Place it on a ground glass plate and moisten with oilstone powder and alcohol and rub it flat by means of a smooth cork, until the desired weakness is abtained, rinse in alcohol and dry.

To temper clicks, ratchets, etc. :

Heat to a cherry red and dip at once into mercurial ointment.

To temper staffs, cylinders, pinions, etc. :

Enclose articles in a brass cylinder, plug tightly, heat to a cherry red and plunge into water. Remove, polish and draw to a blue.

To make a diamond lap or file :

Prepare a plain brass wheel of convenient size, sprinkle on it some fine diamond dust and hammer it in with a smooth-faced hammer. Then burnish it well.

To make a diamond broach :

Prepare a brass broach, dip the point in oil and then diamond dust. Hammer it gently until the dust disapperas. Burnish if necessary.

To make a polishing broach :

Obtain a piece of ivory the desired size, dip it in oil and then diamond dust and proceed to polish.

To remove quicksilver from jewelry :

Anneal the work gently and boil it out in a sulphuric pickle and repeat if necessary.

To stain clock cases :

Infuse nut galls in vinegar in which rusty nails have been soaked. Then apply and let dry.

Paste for cleaning brass :

Oxalic acid	1 oz.
Rottenstone	6 "
Turpentine	2 "
Train oil	2 "

To polish tortoise shell :

Rub with a cloth on which is used a paste of rottenstone and water or use oxide of tin with water.

Imitation of ground glass :

Sulphate of soda	2 ozs.
Beer	16 "

Apply with a brush, and after dry wash clean.

To polish stones :

Grind first on a fine grindstone, then rub with powdered pumice and finish with oxide of tin on leather.

Lathe oil :

Sperm oil	1 oz.
Kerosene oil	4 "

Powder to clean jewelry :

Saltpetre	20 ozs.
Salammoniac	2½ "
Muriatic acid	15 "
Alum	10 "

Pulverized together and apply with a wet cloth.

To ebonize clock cases :

Logwood chips	8 ozs.
Copperas	½ "

Boil the logwood in one gallon of water for half an hour and then add the copperas. Apply while hot. Give three coats.

To solder set rings :

I.

Fill a teacup with wet sand and bury the stone in it. Solder quickly.

II.

Wrap the stone in wet tissue paper and solder on charcoal, with the ring standing up.

To clean files :

First clean with potash and water, then dip in a solution composed of

Water	8 ozs.
Sulphuric acid	3 "
Nitric acid	1 "

Oil well after rinsing.

To straighten pivots :

Remove the temper, fasten the staff in the lathe while revolving and press gently into a hole in a brass plate about the size of the pivot, holding it at right angles to the pivot. Then remove, temper and polish.

To resharpen files :

First clean in warm potash, then rinse and dry. Then dip quickly in nitric acid and wipe off the acid with a piece of rag wound on a stick. This will leave the acid between the teeth, which will eat deeper into the file.

To temper case-springs :

First heat to a cherry red, then dip in water, polish well and draw the temper to a blue. After the third blueing the spring will be in proper condition.

To polish pivots :

Turn the pivot down until it fits the jewel tightly, then dress down with bell metal and rouge and polish with boxwood and lime, moistened with alcohol.

To clean plaster ornaments :

Coat the article with a paste made of starch and let it dry. When thoroughly dry chip it off and the dirt will come with it.

Powder to clean plates :

Prepared chalk	2 ozs.
Rouge	1 "
Rottenstone	½ "

Plate-cleaning powder :

Paris white . . . . 16 ozs.
Carbonate of ammonia . . . 1 "
Water . . . . 4 "

Mix well and apply with chamois skin.

To retain polish on metals :

Wax paraffine . . . . 1 oz.
Petroleum . . . . 3 "

Melt wax and let cool, then add petroleum. Apply with a soft brush.

Resist varnish :

Resin . . . . 2 ozs.
Turpentine . . . . 4 "

To give different shades add red lead, chrome yellow or Prussian blue.

Plate-cleaning powder :

Whiting . . . . 4 ozs.
White oxide of tin . . . . . 2 "
Calcined hartshorn . . . . . 2 "

Reduce to powder and apply with chamois skin.

Solution for testing silverwares :

Nitric acid . . . . 6 ozs.
Water . . . . 2 "
Bichromate of potash . . . . 1 "

Reduce the potash to a powder and well mix with the acid and water and use cold. Keep in glass-stoppered test bottle. File the surface of article first, then apply. If it leaves a blood-red spot it is pure silver ; on German silver it leaves a brown spot ; on Britannia metal a black spot ; on platinum there is no action, and other metals it leaves various colors.

Acid to test gold :

Nitric acid . . . . 2 ozs.
Muriatic acid . . . . 1 scruple.
Water . . . . 4 drachms.

File the article and touch with acid. If it is over 9k gold there will be no effect, but if a lower grade the acid will boil green. If gold be alloyed with silver the mark will be of a paler color.

To renovate tarnished gold:

I.

Bicarbonate of soda	2 ozs.
Salt	1 "
Chloride of lime	1 "
Distilled water	16 "

II.

Sesquioxide of iron	3 ozs.
Calcined borax	2 "
Chloride of ammonia	1 "
Water	2 "

Well mix to a paste and apply with a brush, and afterwards heat gently in a copper pan.

To test gold over 18k:

Muriatic acid	4 ozs.
Nitric acid	2 "
Water	2 "
Salt	½ "

Apply with glass stopper. Will tarnish anything below 18k.

To polish jewel holes:

Polish the hole with a copper broach, oiled and dipped into diamantine, working gently into the jewel hole, the same as if using a brass one.

To prevent iron and steel from rusting:

Boiled linseed oil	1 litre.
Brown varnish	2 "
Turpentine	¼ "
Camphor	45 grains.

Stir well with a wooden stick, boil the solution and allow the article to remain in for a short time.

To satin watch plates:

Procure a fine steel-wire swing scratchbrush and revolve at a high speed. Apply the plates jently, keeping them well moistened with stale beer or potash water.

To grind stones and glass :

Use a fine corundum wheel, running at high speed, and keep well moistened with carbolic acid.   Grind on the side of wheel.

Good paste for polishing nickel :

Lard or tallow . . . . 3 ozs.
Flour emery . . . . 6 "
Melt the lard or tallow and mix in the emery to the consistency of a stiff paste.

To prevent rivets cracking :

When riveting any metal pin or staff, if the head has a tendency to crack, keep it moist with some thick oil and continue hammering.

CHAPTER XI.

REFINING.

What is meant by refining is to render alloys of metals to their pure state, each independently, and it is accomplished by either of the following means, *i. e.*, acids and fusion.

It is very essential and economical for all small or large jobbers and manufacturers to carefully preserve their floor sweeps, polishings, old crucibles, waste waters, etc., in a separate compartment, expressly for that purpose, and let accumulate until sufficient quantity has been obtained to allow the process of refining. Jobbers who are not equipped for this work can always obtain refiner's value by sending it to any of the leading refiners and smelters, which, in case of large quantities would be highly advisable. In such case we can cheerfully and highly recommend Messrs. L. Lelong & Bro., corner of Marshall and Halsey streets, Newark, N. J., as being well equipped for such work, and will, to our knowledge, give full value and satisfaction on receipt of of freight or express, guaranteeing promptness and attention.

We will now describe the two methods of refining which we would highly recommend as being practiced by us in our factory and school, after saying a few words about waste waters.

WASTE WATERS.

The precious metals in waste waters are collected in the following manner: Obtain three good barrels and place them side by side. The first two must be connected with a piece of piping, about six or eight inches from the top, also a piece of piping connecting the second with the third. The bottom of the third barrel is to be drilled with holes of about one-fourth of an inch diameter, and filled about half full with common sawdust. The action then is as follows: All the water, pickle, waste colors, etc., coming directly from the sink or place where they are used enter in the first barrel from the top. When that barrel is as full as the overflow pipe will allow, it passes into the second barrel, therefore naturally leaving a great portion of the sediment at the bottom. The same happens in the second barrel when, after it is full, it passes into the third, where it is well filtered through the sawdust, and passes out lastly as clear water. In the three barrels may be added occasionally a little proto-sulphate of iron or oxalic acid, which will have the effect of immediately precipitating any metallic forms in the waters to the bottom. It is best to dissolve the proto-sulphate of iron (green copperas), in hot water. After the barrels have stood for six months, or thereabouts, the water may be drawn off with a syphon, and the sediments of the three tubs are placed with the floor sweepings, etc., or future refining.

Place the sweeps, etc., in an iron box with a cover and burn them in a furnace for ten hours, which will reduce their bulk and free it from all organic matter. It should then be melted as follows : Take,

Sweeps, etc.	16 ozs.
Carbonate of potash	8 "
Salt	4 "
Salammoniac	2 "

Or—

Sweeps, etc.	8 "
Salt	4 "
Pearl ash	4 "
Red tartar	1 "
Saltpetre	½ "

Place it all together in a large refiner's crucible and melt down into a button. When in a fused condition more of the sweeps may be added from time to time until the crucible will hold no more. If the first of the above formulæ is used, occasionally add a little saltpetre as the process continues, and if it has a tendency to boil over, a little salt should be at once thrown in. Allow the whole to cool and then break the crucible at the bottom and extract the button of metal, which will consist of silver and gold. It must then be treated as follows : Melt this in a new crucible with borax or potash, and while in a molten state pour it into a vessel of water from a height of six or eight feet. This process granulates the metal, which is treated thus: To every ounce of metal add nitric acid 1 oz., and water 2 ozs., and allow to stand for several hours. Then heat the whole gently, after which all but the gold will be dissolved, the gold alone remaining in the form of a dark brown powder. The liquid is then removed, which contains the silver, and fresh nitric acid is then added to the gold and heated again. After the acid has ceased to act the gold remains pure, which should be well washed in hot water and melted for use. If a sheet of copper is then introduced into the liquid containing silver, it will be immediately precipitated upon it, and can afterwards be scraped off and melted for use.

GOLD AND SILVER FILINGS.

Gold and silver filings should always be kept separate from one another, as near as it is possible to do so, when sufficient quantities have accumulated. They may be treated thus: Procure a fine sieve and well sift them. Then pass a magnet through them a few times to extract any iron or steel filings that may be there. Then proceed as follows : Take

Silver dust or gold dust . . . 12 ozs.
Carbonate of potash . . . . . . 2 "
Salt . . . . 1 "

Well mix them together and place in a crucible, putting a layer of salt on the top. Then melt well and add occasionally a little saltpetre while in a state of fusion, also a little more salt. Then allow to cool and break the crucible at the bottom and take out the button of gold, which may have a little alloy of silver and copper with it. This can be disposed of by granulation and treating with nitric acid as before mentioned. If silver, precipitate with a sheet of copper after having dissolved it in nitric acid.

TO REFINE ROLLED GOLD PLATE.

Heat a quantity of aqua regia to about 85° centr. in a porcelain vessel. Then immerse the rolled plate and leave in until every particle of gold is dissolved. Then boil the liquid for a few minutes and filter, then add a small quantity of green vitriol, which will precipitate the gold in the form of a dark brown powder· Then wash in diluted nitric acid and again with hot water. Finally melt the gold in a new crucible with borax and saltpetre and pure gold will be the result.

Can You Read This?

IF SO, WE WILL SEND YOU A FINE IMITATION

✳ Diamond Free! ✳

Hyacinths	Intaglios	Sard Cameos
Emeralds	Mossagates	Tourmalines
Rubies	Peridots	Agatized Wood
Montana Sapphires	Obsidians	Tipfoils
Amethysts	Rosalines	Egyptian Turquois
Nicolos	Tigereyes	
Noble Opals	Enamels	Shell Cameos
	Rock Crystals	Touchstones
Aquamarines	Spinells	Rose Diamonds
Neochrysolites		Enamel Balls
Diamonds	Opalines	Engraved Stones
	Foilbacks	Tip Brilliants
Cameos		
Onyx	Sardonyx	Catseyes
Moonstones	Turquois	Hematites
Pearls	Olivines	Imitation Stones
Agates	Nirenites	Corals
Needle Pyrites	Essonites	Almandines
Yellow Topaz	Smoky Topaz	Garnets
		Orthoclases

INDEX.

FINIS

GENEVA OPTICAL CO.,

67 and 69 Washington Street,

Chicago, U. S. A.

MANUFACTURERS OF GOLD, SILVER AND STEEL

Spectacles and Eyeglasses

IN EVERY FORM.

Trial Lenses, Opthalmoscopes, Prisoptometers,
Lens Measures, and all kinds of Instruments
and Apparatus for Occulists and Op-
ticians in detecting errors of Re-
fraction, Analyzing Lenses
and Machines for Cutting
and Grinding
Lenses.

Prescription and Repair Work done promptly
and accurately.

SEND FOR CATALOGUE.   **ALWAYS AT THE FRONT**